Reflective Collective:
A Rumour of Humour

To Gwynneth,

I hope you enjoy
my first book!

Blessings,

Sue Stone

Reflective Collective: A Rumour of Humour

Reflections and Poems by Sue Stone

iUniverse, Inc.
New York Lincoln Shanghai

Reflective Collective: A Rumour of Humour

iUniverse books may be ordered through booksellers or by contacting:

iUniverse
2021 Pine Lake Road, Suite 100
Lincoln, NE 68512
www.iuniverse.com
1-800-Authors (1-800-288-4677)

ISBN-13: 978-0-595-38919-3 (pbk)
ISBN-13: 978-0-595-83297-2 (ebk)
ISBN-10: 0-595-38919-8 (pbk)
ISBN-10: 0-595-83297-0 (ebk)

Printed in the United States of America

Dedicated to

Mum and Dad
and my sister Carol.

I hold you
in my heart.

Contents

FOR YOUR HEART

Now I See

Lord, I thought I could see
but now that I can
I realise that I could not

Could not see
You
in the beauty of the petals on a flower
in the rain drops glistening on a leaf
in the purity of freshly fallen snow
in the crash of the waves on the sea
in the roar of the wind through the trees

Could not see
You
in the outstretched hand of a friend
who helps to lighten my load
in times of distress
when all seems bleak

Then
You
came to me
and spoke
Your
Truth
and opened the eyes of my heart
now I see Lord
now I see.

You

I see your smile
in my mind
every day

I long to talk
to you
with you

I long to hear
your voice
your laugh

I long to feel
the touch
of your hand

To be with you
to look after you
to share
my life
with you

You will never leave
my mind.

When You Died

When you died,
I died with you.
Outside I existed,
but inside I died.

I could not smile,
could not laugh,
could not talk,
could not sleep,
could not eat.

I just was.

I was plunged
into a black tunnel
of depression.

Nobody could understand
the loneliness,
the isolation,
the pain.

I could not let anyone near.
Because of the wall.

The wall
around the tunnel.

I did not dare
to think,
that I
would live again.

But somehow,
without my knowing,
over endless time,
I did smile,
I did laugh,
I did talk,
I did sleep,
I did eat.

I was me.

A different me.
A me without you.

It can never
be the same again.

But it can be.
It is.

Circles

Life is full of circles.
I travel round them
getting nowhere.

I look at each circle,
analyse each one
to see where I can get off.

To see if I can do something
to make a difference
to anything.

It feels not.
What is the point.

The tallest building
is made from single bricks.

Each small contribution
adds to the bigger picture.

Nothing is meaningless.
Nothing is pointless.

If nothing is gained,
a lesson is learnt.

I could just stop
not bother to try.
It's my choice.

What would be the point
of giving up.

Introspect

Sometimes I can't speak
more than one word.

It's not that I
haven't got anything to say.

It's that I
have so much to say.

Sometimes I think that
if I put my thoughts
into words
it would be
too much.

So sometimes
when I speak
I just speak
one word.

But if you look
into my eyes
you might see
the depths
of my thoughts
and see that I
have more to say.

But it may remain
unspoken.

Estrangement

I wonder where are you
how are you
why you have cut yourself off
how will I know
if you won't tell me

I wonder if you are happy
or sad
how will I know
if you won't tell me

I wonder if you are ill
or are hurting
how will I know
if you won't tell me

Don't you wonder how I am
don't you care
how will you know
if I can't tell you

I wonder if I see you again
would I embrace you
would I tell you I love you
how will you know
if I can't tell you

I wonder if I see you again
would you embrace me
would you tell me you love me
how will I know
if you won't tell me.

Isolation

Isolation is like standing in a desert
shouting
and no one hears.

Isolation is like falling through thin ice
reaching out a hand
and no one sees.

Isolation is like an explosion
in your brain
and no one knows.

Isolation is
wanting someone to understand you
and no one does.

Isolation is
standing in a crowded room
unable to communicate
the point of life
because you don't see the point of life
yourself.

Isolation is an enemy
of your spirit.
Fight it.

Maturity

You invited me into Your garden
when I was a seed.

You watered me with Your Spirit,
You fed me with Your Word,
You nurtured me with Your Love.

I grew into a plant,
my roots grew deeper,
my tiny shoots looked up towards heaven.

You watered me with Your Spirit,
You fed me with Your Word,
You nurtured me with Your Love.

I grew into a sapling,
my roots grew deeper,
my weak branches reached up towards heaven.

You watered me with Your Spirit,
You fed me with Your Word,
You nurtured me with Your Love.

I grew into a tree,
my roots grew deeper,
my strong branches touched into heaven.

Keep me growing.
Deeper into You.
Higher into You.

Hope

Where do I turn
when all hope is gone.

When every path I tread
seems to end in an impenetrable wall.

I look,
in despair
at what we have done
to Your world.

I look,
in despair
at what we do
to each other.

My heart breaks
with sadness.

Where is hope.

Then You speak to me
in a gentle whisper
and tell me to look to You
for hope.

You tell me
that Your heart broke
with sadness
for your children.

And I bow, worthless
at Your feet
and receive
forgiveness, mercy, grace, love.

And I rise
Your precious heir
loved unconditionally.

And I stand
in Your hope
hope in life eternal.

God In Nature

Some people say they can't see God.

They look up at the stars and wonder
where He is.

They gaze at the mountains and wonder
where He is.

They stare at the oceans and wonder
where He is.

They see trees rich with autumn colours and wonder
where He is.

They gaze at intricate myriad flowers and wonder
where He is.

They applaud the creation of new life and wonder
where He is.

Some people say they can't see God.

I wonder why they can't see.

Expectation

Sometimes I think that I
cannot live up to
Your expectation.

Sometimes I feel
like a failure.

Then I remember
that Your expectation
from me
is for my heart.

You have that Lord.

I am never a failure.

God Is There

In deepest thoughts
that no one knows
God is there.

In unspoken words
that can't be said
God is there.

In all the tears
that no one sees
God is there.

In hurt emotions
that can't be shared
God is there.

In painful memories
that take years to heal
God is there.

Take heart.
God is always there.

Diamonds In The Dust

As we rush
through life
we create clouds
of dust

That obscures
the treasures

Of life

It is good
to take time

To stop
and look
through the dust

To see what we
might have missed

There will be
diamonds

Diamonds in the dust.

You Are The Answer

When it feels like I'm walking through a desert
Arid and thirsty
You are the stream that beckons
Saying
Come drink from me
Bathe in me
I will refresh you.

When it feels like I'm climbing life uphill
Tired and struggling
You are the hand that reaches out
Saying
Take hold of Me
I will lift you up
I will guide you.

When it feels like I can't take one more step
Exhausted and dejected
You are the arms that reach out
Saying
I am here
Run to me
I will carry you.

When it feels like I'm on my own
Scared and lonely
You are the voice that whispers
Saying
I will never leave you
Or forsake you
I am with you always.

When it feels like all is darkness
Hopeless and pointless
You are the love that stretches out
Saying
I am the Light of the world
I am big enough for you
Trust in me.

In Silence

In silence
was
Communication

Words unspoken
were conveyed
by the blink of your eyelids
by the look in your eyes
by the movement of your hand
as it sought mine

I think you found strength
that I understood
your thoughts
and
your words
that you
could not speak

I think you found peace
in your faith

I think you found comfort
that you were not alone

In silence

And the bond
grew stronger

In silence
was
Communication

Communication
is never
just words.

Dignity

Dignity
is not about
outward appearance

That is only skin deep

Dignity
is about
Inner strength

When you meet someone
who shows
True dignity
in the face
of adversity

You know
that you have met

Dignity

And it will make
you feel

Humbled.

Loss

Sometimes there are no words
to describe
the anger
that you can feel
with loss

It consumes you

Until it gives way
to sadness

and all you can do
is wait

Until.

Lost Opportunities

The more you mature
the more you realise

The lost opportunities
that have past

For things you should
have said
for things you should
have done

And the more
experience
and
wisdom
you grow into

You realise

That it achieves nothing
regretting
anything past

Because you cannot change it

But you can
learn from it
and build on it

And then you can
move on

And you become
more content

And realise
that your life

Is o.k.

Unspoken Pressure

Unspoken pressure
of conforming
to others

ideas
expectations

of how we should
be living
our lives

of how we should
be behaving

of what they think
we should

be doing
be saying

Sometimes the pressure
is just
in our minds
in our imagination

Sometimes
it is not

Whether it is
or not

We do not
have to conform
to others

We just have
to be true

to ourselves
and our calling

Have the courage
To be yourself.

Unanswered Questions

Where do you go to in your mind
when you have tried every path of thought
that you can think of
and still cannot find any of the answers

That you are looking for
as to the meaning of
anything

You go
nowhere
eventually

Then you start back
at the beginning

And you find that you focus
on one thought
that sheds a ray of hope

And you hold onto that ray

Until the ray grows
into a beam

And the beam grows
into a light

And then there is hope
of some sort

It's a start.

A New Beginning

We walked the path of life together
You were daughter, sister, wife, mother, friend.
You touched so many lives
With your love and joy.

You made our lives so much richer
By just being you.
We will always remember
Your face, your smile, your laugh.

Precious memories will remain in our minds
We will always hold you in our hearts.
Now our hearts are touched with sadness
As we have to say goodbye.

And as you fade from our view
We stand with outstretched arms and say
We love you.

And you walk towards your Creator
Who stands with outstretched arms and says
Welcome home, my precious child, I love you.

FOR YOUR HUMOUR

Camping

Fred said let's go camping,
I said you're off your head,
I can't be doing with that malarkey,
Let's go five star instead.

He said come on, it'll be such fun,
Hiking through nature's best,
I said you can have the wildlife then,
I just want to rest.

He said the air will be so fresh,
It will be lovely for your lungs,
I said I don't like country smells,
I find my nose it bungs.

I just don't like those nasty niffs,
Of all those cows and sheep,
If that's what you call fresh air,
That's something you can keep.

I don't like sleeping on the ground,
Inside a sleeping bag,
It really tries my patience,
And makes me lose my rag.

I don't like the creepy crawlies,
Or all those pesky bugs,
They'll crawl inside my sleeping bag,
And bite me—little thugs.

I don't like cooking on that little stove,
Or eating off of a metal plate,
Or drinking from a metal mug,
You can forget that lark mate.

I don't mind going walking,
But not with a heavy back pack,
I much prefer my handbag,
It's better for my back.

There's never anywhere to wash,
Except inside the tent,
It's always a palaver,
You can only stand up bent.

I want to flick a switch,
And have some instant light,
And have a soak in a nice hot bath,
Now that all sounds just right.

So all in all the answer's no,
I won't go camping Fred,
I much prefer a nice hotel,
And a lovely comfy bed.

Well Fred and me could not agree,
Just how to go and roam,
So in the end it was stalemate,
And we just stayed at home!

Hey Dude

Hey dude,
Who do you think you are,
You think you are so super cool,
Propping up the bar.

With your slicked-back hair,
And your silicone smile,
You think the ladies will come running,
Instead they run a mile.

With your drain pipe trousers,
And fluorescent pink socks,
With button down collar shirts,
And rings as big as rocks.

You tried to chat me up once,
I told you to shove off,
You couldn't see why I didn't say yes,
You thought I was a toff.

You never think it's down to you,
If a girl won't be your date,
As far as you are concerned,
You really are first rate.

I think it's time you grew up,
Got some sense into your life,
Stop thinking you are women's gift,
Or you'll never get a wife.

It's not about the clothes you wear,
It's not about your wealth.
Stop trying to put on a show,
Just try to be yourself.

Let people see you as you are,
It's what's inside that real,
So start to be more honest dude,
And let them see the deal.

Chocolate

My fridge is full of chocolate,
I like it nice and cold,
It never passes its sell by date,
It never gets that old.

Milk or plain,
Black or white,
Anywhere, anyhow,
I'll eat it day or night.

I can eat lots and lots,
I don't get upset tummy,
So don't give it another thought,
Just pass the chocolate bunny.

I don't get spots,
I don't get fat,
So pass more chocolate,
No time to chat.

Don't try to take my chocolate,
It's only meant for me,
Take it and I'll punch your nose,
Try it and you'll see!

Billy

Billy was so super cool,
Or at least that's what he thought,
Even though he was a little plump,
And only four foot short.

We thought we'd like to ask him why,
He thought he was so great,
We reckoned the quickest way for this,
Was to find out from his mate.

Clive was Billy's best mate,
But who would be the one,
To ask Clive to tell us about Billy,
Volunteers—there were none.

So we had to draw the short straw,
To find out who would ask,
As no one would step forward,
To take upon the task.

Betty drew the shortest straw,
Best pleased she didn't look,
We said hard luck you've drawn the straw,
We're not letting you off the hook.

Betty set off to ask of Clive,
Something of Billy's story,
She hoped she would not hear anything,
Which she would think quite gory.

Tell me Clive, Betty started to say,
As her knees began to knock,
Why does Billy think he's cool,
When his hair is quite a shock.

He's fairly short,
He's not so thin,
He's got thick glasses,
And a toothy grin.

He has no dress sense,
His clothes are out of date,
He doesn't seem to notice,
Tell me—you're his mate.

Clive looked a little puzzled,
Then he started to smile,
He said sit down love,
This could take a while.

Clive said Billy's never bothered,
With all the outward things,
Like fancy clothes or new hair styles,
Big watches or gold rings.

He knows these things don't matter,
They're really just for show,
It's what's inside that's important,
I'm surprised you didn't know.

It's being someone's best friend,
Caring when they're sick,
Taking time to know them,
Knowing what makes them tick.

It's letting them know they're special,
Letting them know you care,
Treating them with justice,
Treating them real fair.

It's listening to someone's problems,
Being there when they are sad,
It's laughing with them when they're happy,
Rejoicing when they're glad.

A friend is for you all the time,
They're always on your side,
They sometimes like to give advice,
And sometimes like to guide.

Well Billy is my best friend,
He's always there for me,
He's the best friend anyone could want,
I hope now you can see.

Billy doesn't think he's great,
Although some say that's so,
The only ones who say it,
Are the ones who just don't know.

Billy's confidence comes from within,
And what's within shines out,
Billy's kind and loving,
There really is no doubt.

Betty suddenly felt humbled,
After listening about Billy,
She went back to her friends,
And said she felt quite silly.

We have got it wrong she said,
Billy really is quite cool,
He doesn't care what others think,
That is his golden rule.

He lives his life to help those in need,
He fosters qualities that matter,
He doesn't get involved in trivia,
Or listen to idle chatter.

When Betty finished telling her friends,
They could see Billy was no fool,
From that day forward they looked at him,
And saw him as he really was—cool!

Animals

I think I'd like an animal,
I'm not too sure which one,
Do I want one that sits still,
Or one that wants to run?

Maybe one that's very big,
Or then again quite small,
There are so many to choose from,
I really don't know at all.

Let me consider the options,
And think which one is best,
Then I would know which one to get,
And just leave all the rest.

Dogs would just jump up,
And scratch me on my legs,
The big ones make me wobble,
And unsteady on my pegs.

Cats have such big claws,
To scratch me on my hand,
I'm allergic to them anyway,
When on my lap they land.

What about some fish,
Swimming inside a tank,
But then the tank gets filthy,
And cleaning is so rank.

Birds makes so much noise,
Squawking in their cage,
If I was trying to get some sleep,
It might make me in a rage.

Well I don't think any one will do,
Although they all seem cute,
But each one has its drawbacks,
And not one will really suit.

So if you want an animal,
Get an extra one for me,
But you can look after it,
And take it for a pee.

You can take it for a walk,
In the pouring rain or snow,
Or stand for hours calling it in,
You'd like that now, I know.

You can lug back tins of nosh,
For your little lovely pet,
And pay the astronomical bills,
Given by the vet.

You can mend the furniture,
Which little claws have caught,
And moan at your bank balance,
When a new three piece you've bought.

I think I'll stick to my furry animals,
They're really no trouble to keep,
No feeding or cleaning or walking,
Or disturbing me from my sleep.

I really do like animals,
As long as they don't live with me,
I like them at a distance,
They're cute for all to see.

I sometimes think I'll get a pet,
Then remember why I won't,
If ever you hear me say I might,
Just shout in my ear DON'T!

Next Door's Washing

Sally has a ground floor flat,
She thinks it is so sweet,
She likes to keep it nice and clean,
She likes to keep it neat.

Sally has a problem,
With Madge who lives next door,
Madge has a thing about her washing line,
It really is a bore.

Next door's washing,
Is such a blinking pest,
Dresses, shirts and trousers,
Tea towels, sheets and vests.

Why is it such a pest,
I hear you asking why,
Madge lives on the first floor,
Her washing line is high.

Her washing blocks the sunlight,
From Sally's garden square,
Sally's tried to talk to Madge,
But Madge said she doesn't care.

Madge pegs it out at nine o'clock,
And leaves it out all day,
She takes it in at five o'clock,
Says it's not been in the way.

It doesn't take eight hours to dry,
Two or three would be all right,
She leaves it out on purpose,
It seems just out of spite.

It blocks the light from Sally's plants,
The grass doesn't see the sun,
Sally likes to potter in her garden,
But next door spoils the fun.

Sally can't lay out on her sunbed,
To try to get a tan,
Not when Madge's washing is out,
Sally's not her biggest fan.

Madge doesn't have a garden,
She says it isn't fair,
So she won't consider others,
Those times are very rare.

Madge seems to be quite jealous,
She seems to be quite dour,
She's not a happy person,
She really seems quite sour.

If only Madge would think of others,
She surely would feel more cheery,
She would have lots of friendly chats,
Her life wouldn't be so dreary.

So the moral of this story is,
Don't think only of yourself,
Give and take and lighten up,
It will do wonders for your health!

Trolley Rage

It's time to do the weekly shop
I start off in such a good mood
I head off to the supermarket
to buy myself some food.

As I drive into the car park
I start to get quite narked
I cannot find a single space
as some cars are badly parked.

I finally find somewhere to park
then head towards the door
not in such a good mood now
as I get into the store.

I cannot push my trolley straight
it has such wonky wheels
it has a mind all of it's own
as I'm studying the deals.

Then someone bangs her trolley
smack! into my legs
as I'm turning round the corner
and heading for the eggs.

One second later the same again
into my legs her trolley cruised
I stepped aside, said you go first
as that's both my legs you've bruised.

She strode past looking oh so smug
that isn't so smart I thought
she smashed into the frozen peas
and tears to her eyes it brought.

I hurried past the chocolate
If I stop I'll just buy lots
my dentist really is a nag
your teeth, he says, it rots.

As I turn into the bread aisle
Shelve packers have blocked the way
by leaving huge crates of unpacked goods
right in the middle, and there they stay.

They've gone off for their tea break
and along comes a mindless shopper
who parks their trolley right alongside
and is about to come a cropper.

By now my patience has run out
don't leave it there I shout
it's just as well I don't have gloves
I could go a ten round bout.

I'll leave it there as long as I like
the shoppers reply was tense
I say I'll knock it out the way
if you can't use your sense.

I line up at the checkout
to pay and get my bill
just as it's my turn the cashier says
I'm closed—use another till.

I finally pay and get out quick
glad to get out of the din
I get to the car and can't open the door
as some numbskull has blocked me in

By the time I get home I'm furious
it always takes an age
my good mood never lasts for long
as I suffer from—TROLLEY RAGE!

Getting On

Now that I am getting on
Will life be as much fun
Should I start wearing knitted cardigans
And tie my hair back in a bun

Should I stop going to the gym
In case I take a tumble
And let youngsters shout their views
While I sit back and mumble

Well actually, I like racing round
And letting my hair flow
And working up a sweat in the gym
It gives a healthy glow

And my opinion is just as valid
As the youngsters can express
I like wearing jeans and trainers
It is my sense of dress

Well ageism is nonsense
When all is said and done
So whatever your age just go ahead
And you have lots of fun

I don't think I am ready
To slow down, well not yet
Perhaps one day I'll act my age
But I wouldn't place a bet!

If I Were A Politician

Politics is an interesting subject,
On most things I have a view,
I wouldn't mind having a go,
To see how I would do.

I wonder if I could do better,
I'd put good policies in place,
I'd try to change a lot of things,
And slow down the rat race.

I'd look at education,
What would make the teachers happy,
And keep the parents satisfied,
So no one would get snappy.

I'd look into the police force,
And their powers, then define,
Just what they need to help them,
In their fight against all crime.

Then there's the judicial system,
It needs a good old shake,
And making sure the judges,
Balanced judgements they will make.

Another thing I'd tackle,
Is the dear old National Health,
So everyone gets seen on time,
And it won't depend on wealth.

I'd want to sort pollution,
All sorts, there is a range,
And see what can be put in place,
To bring about a change.

I'd have a look at taxes,
And what we have to show,
And I would make it very clear,
Just where our taxes go.

People need an ambassador,
Someone they know will care,
To champion their corner,
And see we're treated fair.

Then we can say Great Britain,
And really know it's great,
A country to be proud of,
And one that is first rate.

If only I was in parliament,
I'm sure I'd make a stand,
And tackle all the issues,
Now wouldn't that be grand!

Frying Pan Fran

Fran's upstairs' neighbour
He makes such a din
She really did find
That it did her head in

Fran said to him
Ben, are you aware
That your taste in music
I really don't share

Especially at midnight
When I'm trying to sleep
For my ceiling it shakes
And awake I do keep

He just didn't care
About the noise he did make
He was pushing her patience
No more could she take

So she got out her pan
The one used to fry
She lifted it up
And swung it quite high

Fran aimed it at Ben
And she whacked his head
He saw little stars
And his eyes they went red

Fran's usually quite placid
With no temper to show
Which just goes to tell
That you never do know

That make someone angry
And push them about
You might need to watch
'Case they give you a clout

Now Fran's flat is quiet
It was all worth her labour
For Ben's now considerate
And quite a good neighbour!

The Dentist

I went to see my dentist
He said your wisdoms have gone bad
I'll have to take all four out
I said you must be mad

I said I can't go through that much pain
It would make me far too stressed
He said you have no option
It will have to be addressed

So after more debating
And he had much smooth talked
I found that I'd agreed to it
When out of there I walked

Two weeks later I went back
And sat in that black chair
And wondered how I'd got to this
As at the ceiling I did stare

I said you'll have to put me out
He said on that I do intend
I'll give you strong sedation
Then to your teeth I'll tend

I clutched onto that black chair
My knuckles they went white
He said now don't you worry
I know you'll be all right

He said I know what I am doing
It will all go very smooth
Just take it easy and relax
And that to you I'll prove

Before I knew it, he'd done it
My wisdoms were all out
I didn't feel a twinge of pain
I didn't even shout

So now my teeth are perfect
Even though it took a while
But now it feels much better
And I have a lovely smile

I don't miss my wisdoms
They really were a pain
Sometimes it is true to say
That a loss can be a gain

So if you need a dentist
And you drop me a line
I'll be happy to send you
The name and address of mine

I really think he's very good
One of the best I've seen
And for me that's saying something
Because on dentists I'm not keen

He doesn't know I eat lots of sweets
And loads of chocolate too
So if you go and see him
Keep that between me and you!

Ice Cream Eric

Eric, he sold ice creams
He was a lonely man
He wished he had a girlfriend
But he only had a van.

His van was always sparkling white
And on top was a giant cone
With strawberry coloured pink ice cream
And the song it played would drone.

He travelled round the neighbourhood
Selling his ice cream
His longings for a girlfriend
Were only but a dream.

Just as he'd all but given up
Of finding love so true
He happened to meet Cheryl
It was out of the blue.

He looked at her all tongue tied
He couldn't think what to say
Then Cheryl said hurry up mate
I haven't got all day.

Will you go out with me he said
She said have you gone mad
I only wanted an ice cream
Although you don't look bad.

She said I'll meet you tonight then
Eric's heart was all a flutter
He gave Cheryl three scoops of her fav
Choc-chip and brandy butter.

They got on so very well
Before long the knot they tied
They were quite inseparable
They were always side by side.

If you hear the sound of bells
And it's Eric the ice cream man
You will see them happy together
Both in the ice cream van.

The Opticians

I went to the opticians,
For him to test my sight,
He said sit down on that chair dear,
And look into this light.

My eyes had not adjusted,
After stepping from sunlight,
Into the darkened eye test room,
Which was as dark as night.

And after he'd half blinded me,
With the light that was so strong,
He asked me lots of questions,
Which I tried not to get wrong.

He said are you having problems,
I said not that I can tell,
He said look straight ahead now,
You're doing very well.

He fixed some heavy glasses on,
Tucked them behind my ears,
They really were uncomfortable,
I thought thanks for that mate, cheers.

He said sit right back in that chair,
Forward you can't lean,
Which circle is the brighter,
The red one or the green.

I said I cannot really tell,
They look the same to me,
He said well they are not my dear,
Look closer and you'll see.

He changed the lenses over,
And said which one is best,
I said hold on, you go so fast,
It feels like a speed test.

My eyes, they were o.k. this time,
I was relieved to hear,
As I didn't want to buy new specs,
Because they are so dear.

I always get so nervous,
I just don't like the test,
I come out quite exhausted,
And go home for a rest.

At least then it is over,
For another year or two,
And considering it is some ordeal,
Aren't you glad it wasn't you?

Ned And Me

I had a horse ride
Through the green countryside
I thought we would trot
But my horse he thought not

He decided to run
Thought it would be fun
We headed for trees
Giving me wobbly knees

As he started to race
Branches whacked on my face
My hair it did fly
And my lips they went dry

I thought if we stop
I'll go over the top
He thinks it's a race
And he's setting the pace

When he finally slowed down
I said Ned, you're a clown
I think I'll walk back
'Cos you've got the sack

You've made my nerves bad
That's the worse time I've had
While out on a horse
Over such a short course

I'll not choose you again
'Cos you've caused me some pain
So don't look with surprise
In your lovely big eyes

That say try me again
And I think you will gain
I'll show you I'm good
As we go through the wood

So I tried Ned next day
And I have to say
He did as was told
He was good as gold

So now Ned's the one
That I choose for a run
We're good friends are we
My old Ned and me.

You Never Buy Me Flowers

Why don't you buy me flowers,
I said to Stan, my bloke,
He said I can't afford it,
Because I'm always broke.

I said well don't be mingy,
That's no way to win my heart,
Put your hand into your pocket,
And with a few pounds part.

I said just buy a little bunch,
The cost wouldn't be that great,
And I would really like them,
And very much appreciate.

So he went out and bought some,
He said they were quite cheap,
I said I'm not surprised Stan,
They're fit for the rubbish heap.

He said if you're going to criticise,
I won't bother any more,
I said perhaps you shouldn't then,
If you think it's such a chore.

Next day he went out again,
More flowers he did clutch,
He said what do you think of these,
I said, frankly Stan, not much.

But at least you've made an effort,
I said it with good cheer,
But if you buy me more dead blooms,
I'll wrap them round your ear!

In Favour Of The Blues

My brother he likes football,
He has a season ticket,
My knowledge only goes as far,
As they have a goal and not a wicket.

His team they play in blue,
You can probably guess their name,
They always seem to do so well,
And win most cups in the game.

I know they all run round like mad,
One way and then the other,
And if one of them should score a goal,
They all jump on and smother.

I've noticed they fall down a lot,
And then they start to moan,
And if it goes on for too long,
The crowd they start to groan.

They make up songs to take the mick,
Out of the other side,
And sing in great loud voices,
As their opponents they deride.

I'm sure they didn't play so much,
Back in days gone by,
It's never off the tele now,
I really don't know why.

I went to see a game once,
About thirty years has past,
And if I wait another thirty more,
That won't be a day too fast!

Handy Man

I know a chap called Eddie,
He is a handy man,
If he can't do the job himself,
He'll know someone who can.

If you need a wall built,
With cement nice and thick,
If Ed can't build the wall himself,
He'll call in Rick the Brick.

Rick hasn't got a level eye,
His walls are not that straight,
But he is well aware of this,
So works for a low rate.

Ed knows a chippie called Everett,
His name's too long to say,
So everyone calls him Ever,
As he always takes all day.

If you need something painted,
Or paper hung on a wall,
Ed will probably do it,
If not, he'll call in Paul.

The only thing with Paul is,
The poor chap's colour blind,
If you ask for red you might get green,
So don't use him if you'll mind.

Ed knows a plumber called Larry,
I called him in one week,
To tell the truth, he wasn't that good,
I named him Larry the Leak.

Joseph is an electrician,
He's really not that bright,
He can't do much that's complicated,
But he can wire in a light.

Well actually, they're a motley bunch,
I think I'll try the jobs on my own,
And not only will I save some cash,
I won't have to listen to them moan!

My Favourite Diet

I wouldn't mind a diet
If only one would let
Me eat sweets and chocolate
But I haven't found one yet

I couldn't give up roasties
Or biscuits nice and sweet
And cream cakes are so lovely
They really are a treat

And then of course there's fry ups
And lovely big fat chips
With lots of runny ketchup
That runs all down your lips

And I really like desserts
Any kind at all
With lots of lovely ice cream
Piled up nice and tall

Crisps, peanuts and fizzy drinks
And lots of tasty snacks
It's hard not to indulge in these
When you're trying to relax

If someone could invent a diet
That includes all that and more
They would sell so many books
They could retire, that's for sure!

Gregory

I don't know why I see you
Sometimes you're not much fun
And who wants to have a boring time
When all is said and done

We just sit and watch the tele
While to go out I do long
But sometimes you can make me laugh
And in my heart you put a song

So I'll stick by you Gregory
But you must do your part
And if my bloke you want to be
Then try to win my heart

'Cos if you don't I'll dump you
And go out with someone new
There are a lot to choose from
I've been asked by quite a few

This is your last chance Gregory
To see what you can do
Try to whisk me off my feet
Or it's the chop for you!

Adverts — What Adverts?

Is it just me who thinks adverts
Can be somewhat obscure
Just what they aim to advertise
I really can't be sure

I always try to guess
When I see one that's new
But until the last second
I usually haven't got a clue

If only they were obvious
So we can clearly tell
Without a shadow of a doubt
What they are trying to sell!

Spaghetti Bolognese

Can anyone eat spaghetti bolognese
And not end up in a mess
With orange blobs on their face
And orange blobs down their dress?

The blobby bits are not so bad
It's the spaghetti that's the trick
Trying to wrap it round my fork
It just gets on my wick

It slips about all over the place
One way and then the other
By the time you finally capture it
In sauce it will you smother

I haven't yet mastered the art
Of eating it and staying clean
I'm not the only one though
Many others I have seen

And no one likes others to see
Them getting in a state
It always looks more polite
If your dinner's on your plate

So if I'm doing dinner
And spag bol I am cooking
I make a point of eating it
When no one else is looking!

Happy Holidays

I'm going on my holidays,
At last the time has come,
I'm off to where the sun shines bright,
Relaxation, to get some.

I'm going to go swimming,
In the sea so blue,
And float around so lazy,
'Til the sun it sets it's hue.

I'm going to lay out in the sun,
And get myself a tan,
And drink as many ice cold drinks,
As I think I can.

I'll try out all the water sports,
And trips, I'll try a few,
I'm going to explore around,
And see something that's new.

There'll be lots of people there,
That I don't know at all,
Folks are always friendly,
I think I'll have a ball.

I'll sip champagne at evening time,
Eat my share of fancy nosh,
With waiter service, what a change,
I'll dress up really posh.

And before I know, it will be time to pack,
It will make me a bit sad,
But although I always enjoy my hols,
To get back I'm always glad!

Staying In Trim

Oh isn't it grim
When your bod's not in trim
And your belly does sag
Like an old carrier bag

With thighs like tree trunks
Still more biscuits you dunk
You know that you shouldn't
But then, well who wouldn't

You go jogging at dawn
Accompanied by yawn
The going gets tough
And you huff and puff

Your face goes all red
And you're filled with dread
When you realise with woe
You've still ten miles to go

You get back in a heap
And you just want to sleep
But you go off to work
Where they don't let you shirk

But after a week
In the mirror you peek
And your body's more lean
Then you feel more keen

To keep up with runs
And cut out the buns
'Til you're looking just great
It was all worth the wait!

I Was Never Good At Netball

I was never good at netball,
Although I liked the game,
The odds were stacked against me,
Which was really quite a shame.

I had to play in goal defence,
When I was four foot eleven,
Unfortunately the goal attack,
Her height was six foot seven.

I really didn't stand a chance,
As I jumped to get the ball,
Because she always got there first,
With no effort at all.

I might well have been good at it,
If the odds had been better for me,
But I packed it up, called it a day,
And joined the team for hockey!

My Lethal Hockey Stick

I was very good at hockey,
I always played right inner,
I managed to score loads of goals,
Every one a winner.

I charged around, I knew no fear,
My stick sought out the ball,
I whacked it hard and scored a goal,
With no trouble at all.

My energy it knew no bounds,
I ran around lightning quick,
Everyone got out the way,
For I was lethal with my stick!

Running Away

I'm running away
Got my hat and my coat
I'm going to find
Somewhere more remote

Where no one will nag
Or ask me to do
Millions of tasks
Instead of a few

For I am now flagging
My bones they do tire
And the jobs they still pile up
As I wade through the mire

So I'll find me somewhere
Where I'll have lots of space
Where I can take time out
From this old rat race

And no one will find me
While I have a break
And sit with my feet up
And eat lots of cake!

978-0-595-38919-3
0-595-38919-8

Printed in the United Kingdom
by Lightning Source UK Ltd.
109619UKS00001B/313-408